the ROSE theatre

an archaeological discovery

the ROSE theatre

an archaeological discovery

Julian Bowsher

Foreword by Ian McKellen
Postscript by C. Walter Hodges

First published in Great Britain in 1998 by
Museum of London
150 London Wall, London, EC2Y 5HN

Distributed to the book trade throughout the world by
Art Books International
1 Stewart's Court, 220 Stewart's Road, London, SW8 4UD, UK

British Library Cataloguing-in-Publication data:
a CIP catalogue record for this book is available from
the British Library.

ISBN 0 904818 75 6

Edited, designed and typeset by
ALDINO™
P O Box 207, Abingdon, Oxfordshire OX13 6TA

Set in Adobe Poppl-Laudatio and Apollo

Colour originated by Essex Colour
Printed and bound by The White Dove Press

Contents

Introduction

THE DISCOVERY AND EXCAVATION of the Rose theatre was one of the most exciting archaeological projects of recent years. The Rose was one of the earliest and most successful playhouses of its type, and is historically unique because of the preservation of day-to-day accounts kept by its owner, Philip Henslowe (1555–1616). The excavations were to arouse great interest within the archaeological, historical and theatrical worlds[1].

Southbridge House, the existing 1950s office block on the site, was due to be demolished in 1988. Rescue excavation was needed before redeveloping the site because the Rose was known to have been built there, although it was not known how much of it might have survived beneath the later building. In addition, there was the possibility of uncovering even earlier remains. The Department of Greater London Archaeology of the Museum of London (now superseded by the Museum of London Archaeology Service) began the excavations on 19 December 1988, directed by Julian Bowsher. Initially they were to be for a period of two months, but the importance and general interest of the discovery of the Rose led to an extension of the excavation until 14 May 1989. As the magnitude of the operation increased, as many as twenty-one people were working on the site and Simon Blatherwick joined Julian Bowsher as co-director in April 1989[2].

Construction work on the foundations of a new development on the site was to begin on 15 May but a public outcry, prompted by concern over the remains of this unique monument, led to a postponement and then to a change of plan in building operations. Between June and July 1989 smaller areas of the site, those due to be disturbed by the altered building plans, were excavated by the Central Excavation Unit (now the Central Archaeology Service) of English Heritage under the direction of John Hinchliffe. In order to preserve the remains, the site was sealed with sand and a thin layer of concrete into which monitoring points were inserted, under the supervision of English Heritage conservators, to check on the buried ground conditions. The new development, Rose Court, was completed in June 1991 and incorporates a basement space which has been built over the theatre's remains.

The Rose Theatre Trust was formed in late 1989 in order to ensure that the Rose remains would be re-excavated, preserved and displayed to the public. In February 1992 the site was formally scheduled by the Department of the Environment (as Scheduled Monument 20851) under the terms of the Ancient Monument and Archaeological Areas Act of 1979.

This book begins with a historical summary of London's theatres and a brief history of the Rose itself. However, the text is principally concerned with the results and interpretations of the archaeological excavations. The book does not pretend to be comprehensive in its discussion, but it does attempt to illustrate the importance of the Rose findings for the development of theatre history, and the last chapter sketches the evidence of contemporary performances revealed by the excavations. The Postscript by C. Walter Hodges discusses how, based on the archaeological evidence, the superstructure of the Rose might have appeared in its heyday. However, it must be stressed that this book is a preliminary account based on the evidence available to date. Further research or excavation may alter these views.

Modern archaeological measurements, and ground levels above Ordnance Datum (OD) or sea level, are normally given in metres. However, for convenience and because of the historical context, the equivalent imperial measurements are quoted (in parentheses).

[12] E. Malone, 'An historical account of the English stage' in *The Plays and Poems of William Shakespeare*, vol. I, part 2, London, 1790.

[13] Reproduced in R. A. Foakes and R. T. Rickert, *Henslowe's Diary: edited with supplementary material, introduction and notes*, Cambridge University Press, Cambridge, 1961. Muniment 22, pp306ff.

[14] Such is clear from the surviving building contract. W. W. Greg, *Henslowe Papers: being documents supplementary to Henslowe's Diary*, Oxford University Press, Oxford, 1931. Muniment 49, pp19–22.

[15] A persuasive argument against Vitruvian design is by S. P. Cerasano 1989 (page 10, note 2). Samuel Kiechel in 1585 recorded three galleries (cited in E. K. Chambers 1923, vol. II, p358). Three are also specified in the Fortune (W. W. Greg 1931, Muniment 22, p5, line 20) and Hope (ibid, Muniment 49, pp20–21) contracts. The drawing of the Swan Theatre also shows three galleries. Paul Hentzner in 1598 recorded the playhouses built of wood (cited in J. D. Wilson, *Life in Shakespeare's England*, Penguin, Harmondsworth, 1949, p207) and Thomas Platter in 1599 noted that playing was on a raised platform (cited in E.K. Chambers 1923, vol. II, p365).

[16] *The London Archaeologist*, vol. 6, no. 5, Winter 1989, p140; *Current Archaeology* (art. cit. page 10, note 2), and more comprehensively in S. Blatherwick and A. Gurr, 'Shakespeare's factory', *Antiquity*, vol. 66, no. 251, June 1992, pp315–33.

[17] Cited in G. E. Bentley, *The Jacobean and Caroline Stage*, Oxford University Press, Oxford, 1941–68, vol. II, p690 and passim for a history of the last days of these theatres.

Bankside

THE EARLIEST THEATRICAL AREA in London was Shoreditch, where the Theatre and Curtain were situated and where many actors lived. This was only about an hour's walk to the Bankside, in Southwark, the district of London which came to have the greatest concentration of playhouses. The borough of Southwark was at the southern end of London Bridge, astride a major route from the capital. To the west of the bridge an embankment built along the riverfront became the highway called Bankside. The area of the same name is taken to extend south from the river to Park Street and from Paris Gardens in the west to Bankend in the east.

There had been some development along the river front by the time the Domesday Book was compiled in 1086, when the area was designated a 'Liberty' of autonomous monastic land. In 1127 it became part of the manor of the Bishops of Winchester and became known as the Liberty of the Clink after the Bishops' infamous prison. The area was also within the parish of St Saviour's Church (now Southwark Cathedral). Owing to the Liberty's proximity to London and to its lax regulations, the river front 'stews' developed into a series of inns, gambling dens and brothels. One of these was the Rose inn, situated to the west of a pathway which took its name, Rose Alley, from the inn[1]. Maiden Lane (now Park Street) to the south probably owes its name to the brothels along the river front.

Most of the area was low-lying marshland, liable to flooding and occupied only by market gardens and fishponds. By the sixteenth century development was spreading south from the river front, and animal baiting rings appeared in the 1540s. This 'sport' was to remain popular here until well into the seventeenth century. There was an injunction against 'common players who haunt the Bankside'[2] in 1545, by which time clearly the whole area had become a centre of entertainment. Towards the end of the century the playhouses arrived, providing a new source of amusement but adding to the area's poor reputation. Nevertheless it prospered, and watermen

THE ROSE THEATRE

are recorded as making a good living ferrying wealthier revellers across the river. Shaftesbury Avenue, with its theatres and sundry other entertainments, is the closest parallel that modern London is able to offer.

The Rose was the first theatre to be built in this area, and its location was known long before the excavations began. It is clearly depicted on contemporary maps north of Maiden Lane, although a little farther north than its true position, east of Rose Alley. Numerous documentary records provide detailed evidence for its location.

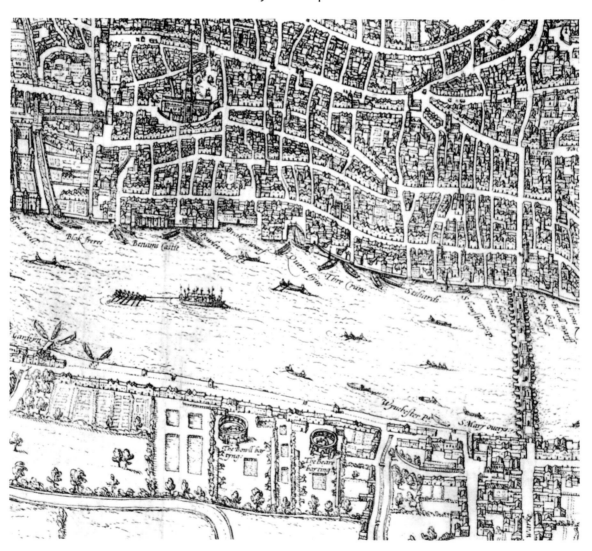

To the west of Rose Alley was an estate called the Rose, while to the east there was another known as the Little Rose, both named after the alley and originally the inn. The Little Rose estate was defined, on later property deeds, as lying between Rose Alley and what is now Southwark Bridge Road, and north of Maiden Lane but some 50m (164ft) short of the river. The present property boundary lies much within the same estate. The earliest mention of the estate dates back to 1552, the year in which it was given to the parish of St Mildred's in Bread Street, London[3].

A detail of the Bankside showing the Rose, marked as 'The play howse', from John Norden's map of London published in Speculum Britanniae, *the first part, London, 1593.*

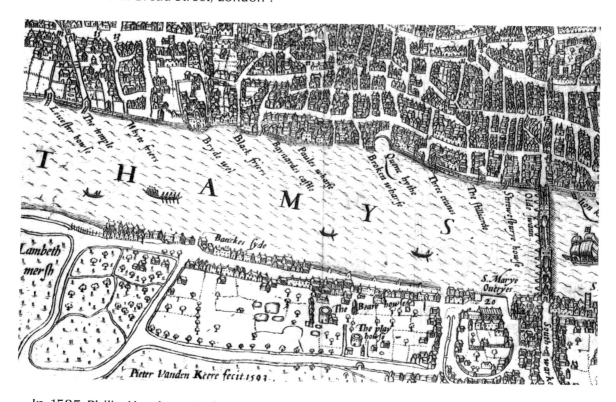

In 1585 Philip Henslowe took out a twenty-year lease on the estate, described as a tenement with two gardens[4]. In his partnership agreement made in 1587 (see next chapter), reference is made to one 'garden plotte', on which the theatre was now being built, that measured 'ffoorescore and fourteene foote' (28.65m/94ft) square[5]. This was clearly the southernmost of the two gardens, as annual records of the Surrey and Kent Commission of Sewers refer to the playhouse being adjacent to its sewer or wharf on the north side of Maiden Lane[6]. These 'sewers', as marked on contemporary maps on each side of Maiden Lane and along Rose Alley, were drainage channels rather than open sewers in the modern sense.

Surprisingly, the exca
any means to support a
a covering would have
upper galleries to each
of one shingle tile four
described has no imme
there may have been

An important feature
house'. Here, the acto
rest and rehearse betw
stored in an upper roc
evidence that the tiring
in the Swan drawing,
a separate structure t
the Rose, the tiring-h
frame of the building
served as the back of
the stage in betwee
used as a tiring-hou
appear to be angled
modern building ac

Disturbance caus
ground in between
the stage, was surfa
found elsewhere,
have been below
have been connec

Left: *a painting by June Everett of the Rose theatre excavations in May 1989. This view shows the beginning of the new building work just to the north of the theatre remains.*

when Henslowe and Cholmley contracted John Grigge to 'ereckte fynishe and sett upp ... the saide play house'[4].

The plot was restricted by the northern and southern ditches and by Cholmley's house to the south-west. The evidence revealed so far suggests that this phase was a simple but irregular polygon with an external diameter of about 22m (72ft). The regularity of the design was broken at the southern end, where the angle of the walls was shown to be shallower than those elsewhere. This foreshortening of the design would have provided an almost straight side along the street frontage.

*A photograph sh
slope of the mor
surface towards
front. The brick
of the first stage
seen, as well as
footings of the :
front in the bac
The modern cc
can be clearly :*

The ground level in between the original gallery walls to the side of the stage was substantially raised and shallow trenches for the new inner wall appeared at this level. This area probably had been the location of the lords' rooms in Phase I and the new surface here was also partially plastered, suggesting continuation of use for this purpose. Henslowe recorded payment for 'sellynge' or sealing the lords' rooms in 1592[27] and this surface treatment, albeit below the wooden gallery floors, may also be associated with the rooms' position. Further support for their location here may be sought in an examination of the same area depicted in the drawing of the interior of the Swan. Here the ground floor gallery to the (viewer's) left of the stage is marked 'orchestra', which is thought to relate to lords' rooms or boxes. Also, in the building contract for the Hope of 1613, there are 'Boxes in the *lowermost* storie fitt and decent for gentlemen to sitt in'[28].

Immediately in front of this area (just to the east) were three flagstones resting on a layer of clay which covered the original inner wall. These would appear to have formed a platform or foundation, but they in turn were sealed by the new yard floor and their purpose remains enigmatic.

Although the southern half of the building remained substantially unchanged, two more brick walls were inserted in between the (original) gallery walls to the south-west. These two walls were definitely constructed after the central cross-wall and clearly belong to Phase II. The surviving fragments are parallel to each other, within the same construction cut, 1.6m (5ft 3in.) apart, and built against the outer wall on each side of one of the pads. This would preclude any association with the exterior of the building. The material found laid between these walls was the same as that of the new yard surface, and also covered a short stretch of the inner wall at this point. This near-intrusion of the yard into the galleries can best be explained as a newly-made entrance from the yard into the galleries, in a similar position to that of the *ingressus*, or internal entrance, shown in the drawing of the Swan. A sketch on the back of a letter from Henslowe to Alleyn, which is dated September 1593, also appears to show such an entrance way[29].

The new stage was built 2.1m (6ft 10½in.) farther north than the original. It had a depth of 5.6m (18ft 4in.) and it is estimated to have been 8.4m (27ft 7in.) long, although its front length was not fully uncovered by our excavation. This would have provided a complete stage area of about 50.5m² (543.58sq ft). The front wall of this stage

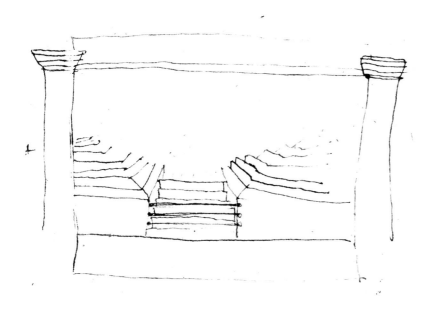

An ingressus *or entranceway, sketched on the back of a letter from Henslowe to Alleyn, dated 28 September 1593. Note the similarity to the* ingressus *in the drawing of the Swan.*

Brickwork forming the pillar base at the western end of the Phase II stage. The timber base plate underneath can also be seen, and the stage front wall to the right.

was built out of mortared chalk blocks and the surviving top was flush with the new yard and sub-stage surfaces on each side of it. As such, perhaps it was also the foundation for a wooden construction of a similar height to that of the first stage. Although its dimensions were not much larger than those of the first stage, it was slightly more rectangular and gave the impression of a greater 'thrust' because of the extension of the yard on each side of it.

The relationship of the new wall at the back of the stage to the new inner wall around the yard has been lost; only some stakes appeared on the same alignment. The foundations of this back wall had been made of brick rubble, strengthened by stakes within a trench distinctly deeper than the inner wall foundations. This foundation was curved, but straight stretches of a brick superstructure survived in the centre. This indicates that the facade or *scenae frons* of the stage was divided into three flat planes similar to its predecessor but with shallower angles, and more formalised.

Above the organic accumulation over the first stage surface of the playhouse a number of fills were laid down to raise the ground level, mostly deposited after the construction of the new stage front. This area was then given a homogenous surface of compacted earth.

Just inside the line of the stage front were the remains of two pillar bases. These were at each end of the stage, 6.5m (21ft 4in.) apart measured centre to centre. The base to the east was partly destroyed by modern piles but the western one was fully preserved. This was a brick plinth resting on a timber base plate. The timber was placed on a chalk scree laid over the organic accumulation of the first stage surface but laid up against the new stage wall, and therefore clearly formed part of the Phase II building. These bases would have supported pillars extending up through the stage boards, thus supporting a 'cover' or roof over the playing area.

The addition of this roof was clearly associated with the relocation of the galleries on each side of the stage, in order to accommodate sightlines from the upper floors. The position of the original galleries in this area would have prevented any view of the stage from their upper storey, if there had been a roof over it. Demolition debris in the yard in front of this stage indicates that its roof was tiled with wooden shingles and that the ceiling itself had been constructed of lath and plaster[30]. In 1592 Henslowe had recorded payment for 'payntinge my stage' and the Swan is also documented as having been cleverly painted[31].

A thin depression line within the new yard surface 1.3m (4ft 3in.)

in front of, and parallel to, the stage wall indicated that the stage roof projected beyond the edge of the stage but was not guttered.

It was perhaps in 1592 that the 'hut' was added above the rear of the stage. Although it is absent in Norden's first map, it is seen in both the map and, more clearly, the panorama which are dated to 1600. There it is shown as a small gable seemingly built flush against the main frame. This contrasts with that seen at the Swan which extends beyond the frame, although it may not have extended so far as indicated in the drawing on page 80.

The earthen surface below the Phase II stage covered the inner wall behind the first stage, but not the inlet into the timber drain at the rear. Indeed, the foundation cut of the new back wall of this second-phase stage respected the western side of the drain. The probability remains that any further excavation to the east of the drain would reveal the continuance of this wall. The drain was still in service but if the same inlet was used, its vertical member would have run down the stage facade. A ditch inside and parallel to the new back wall is unexplained, but may also have been connected with the drain.

The extension of the galleries to the side(s) and of the stage to the north resulted in a larger yard, the complete area of which was increased by approximately thirty-nine per cent to cover about 163m² (1754½sq ft), and the effect of greater thrust to the stage.

Within the confines of the original inner wall circuit, dumps of earth levelled out the rake of the previous floor. The surface of the new yard therefore had to have been at a much higher level than that of the first yard, as it needed to cover the base of the earlier stage and inner walls next to it. Although this floor was not raked, there was a gentle slope of 0.2m (7¾in.) from the southern end to the northern end, where it was laid against the new stage wall. Next to the internal wall to the south-west, there was another depression line within this surface area, of similar dimensions to that in front of the stage, which suggests the continued absence of guttering along the gallery eaves.

The old mortar floor had been quite friable, whereas the new yard surface was made of earth greatly compacted with cinder and cracked hazelnut shells[32]. Material found within this layer, which can therefore be dated before February 1592, included dress pins, leather shoes and a gold finger ring. This surface was certainly more durable and perhaps afforded better drainage too, although how that was achieved is not fully understood.

*Gold finger ring, inscribed
PENCES POVR MOYE DV.
This early French translates
as 'think of me'; DV stands
for Deus Vult, God willing.
Found within the material
forming the surface of the
Phase II yard.*

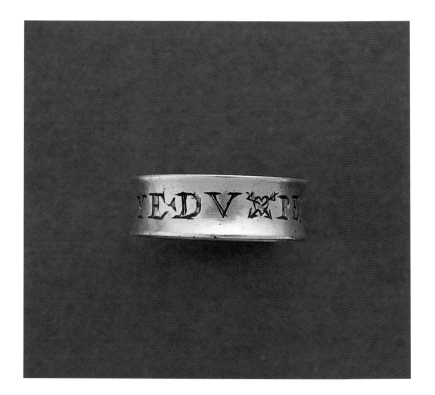

Notes

[1] Both quotes, R. A. Foakes and R. T. Rickert 1961 (page 16, note 13), Muniment 16, line 15, p305.

[2] S. Blatherwick, 'Report on a watching brief at the south end of Southwark Bridge, Park Street, London SE1', unpublished Museum of London Archaeology Service report, July 1991.

[3] cf. page 21, note 5.

[4] R. A. Foakes and R. T. Rickert 1961, Muniment 16, line 22, p305.

[5] R. A. Foakes, *Illustrations of the English Stage 1580–1642*, Scolar Press, London, 1985, pp24-25.

[6] as page 26, note 5; John Orrell, 'Building the Fortune', *Shakespeare Quarterly*, vol. 44, no. 2, Summer 1993, pp128-130.

[7] A polygon could also be measured out from the centre using an isoceles triangle, see F. J. Hildy, 'If you build it they will come: the reconstruction of Shakespeare's Globe gets underway on the Bankside in London', reproduced as Appendix 3 in *The Design of the Globe*, International Shakespeare Globe Centre, London, 1993, pp89–106. The development of the *ad quadratum* system is discussed in eg John Orrell 1983 (page 15, note 9), p115ff.

[8] W. W. Greg 1931 (page 16, note 14), Muniment 22, p5, lines 18–20.

[9] ibid, Muniment 49, p21, lines 53–55.

[10] ibid, Muniment 22, p5, lines 16–17. The measurements quoted above for the Rose are centre to centre, because of the variable thickness of the respective walls, whereas the recorded measurements for the Fortune are calculated from the outer extremity of the outer wall to the inner extremity of the inner wall, as 3.97m (12ft 6in.). The comparable measurement for the Rose is 3.9m (12ft 3in.).

[11] SKCS f422v (29 Aug 1605), both quotes, the second precedes the first.

[12] W. W. Greg 1931, Muniment 22, p5, lines 20–23.

[13] S. Loengard 1983 (page 15, note 2), p309.

[14] See the discussion in D. A. Latter, 'Sight-lines in a conjectural reconstruction of an Elizabethan playhouse', *Shakespeare Survey*, vol. 28, 1975, pp125–135.

[15] 'Leaft above in the tier-house in the cheast'; R. A. Foakes and R. T. Rickert 1961, p319, line 45; C. C. Rutter 1984 (page 26, note 3), Doc. 65, p133, line 26, n. 3.

[16] R. A. Foakes and R. T. Rickert 1961, f5v, p13.

Details showing tapered stage fronts, from the frontispieces of (left) Roxana (1632) by William Alabaster, and (right) Messalina (1640) by Nathanael Richards.

the level of the yard floor, the headroom within this understage space would have been more than a little cramped, especially if access was needed through a trap door.

The absence of a roof over the Phase I stage has also provided a re-evaluation of contemporary performances, for there must have been a few cancellations owing to severe rain. The addition of a roof over the second stage would have corrected this, as well as providing some protection from the sun in the summer. The roof shown on the Swan drawing does not appear to have covered as much of its stage as that at the Rose did. When the Boar's Head inn was adapted for playing in 1598 there does not seem to have been a roof over the stage area, but when it was rebuilt in the next year the addition of such a roof had been seen to be an advantage[11].

The slope of the yard floor of Phase I was a logical design, enabling a greater view from the rear. This was an unexpected feature since the floor of the Swan yard, depicted in 1596, is described by De Witt as level. If this original slope had been designed with the intention of facilitating drainage, it may have turned out to be a mistake, for the second yard floor was distinctly more level.

It is most probable that the alterations of Phase II were primarily associated with a desire to cater for new stage practices that were demanded by an insatiable clientèle as well as by the playwrights. The increase in audience capacity, as a bonus, was a consequence of the new stage arrangements rather than the other way round. It is also clear that the welfare of the actors was considered here; the new stage roof afforded better protection, while the addition of the penthouse shed may have provided larger working facilities. Henslowe's avaricious reputation should be modified in the light of the Rose findings. The first two months of 1592 also saw some 'further building and reparacions' at the Theatre, and although no details of this work are known[12], it would seem that Henslowe was not alone in creating theatrical improvements.

It is with the construction of this phase that economy seems to have been a concern. Although piles had not been used in Phase I, the original foundations were certainly deeper and more substantial than those constructed for Phase II. Some documentary evidence suggests that the Fortune had piled foundations but that the Hope did not[13]. There is still insufficient evidence for the development of playhouse foundations to be discussed.

Although it appears that thatch was probably used from the outset, the only deposits of the material came from destruction layers associated with the second phase. This would seem to contradict Thomas Platter's account of 1599 which implies that the Globe was the only thatched playhouse in the area. Norden's 1600 map indicates thatch on the Rose and Globe, whereas both the Fortune and the Hope contracts specify tiles[14].

While the evidence revealed so far has produced a wealth of information it has also raised almost as many questions, and if there should be any future excavations, a number of points could be clarified. Most importantly the eastern side of the theatre remains to be uncovered, to confirm the dimensions suggested to date. Excavation there might also explain hitherto puzzling features encountered to the west. It is to be hoped that the true extent of the second phase might be revealed, as the north-eastern part already examined proved particularly complicated. There are also areas within the original limits that were not fully examined, and further excavation there would clarify many matters. If deep enough, it might throw further light on the history of the site immediately before the construction of the Rose.

Notes

[1] A left femur, showing butchering and teeth marks, came from a pile shaft to the west, and a skull from a modern demolition pit to the north. Bear bones were also found in excavations at Skinmarket Place, 100m (328ft) to the west of the Rose excavations; Museum of London archive report, SIP 88.

On bearbaiting rings see W. W. Braines 1924 (page 21, note 3) pp90–98; C. L. Kingsford, 'Paris Garden and the bear baiting', *Archaeologia*, 2nd series, vol. 20, 1920, pp155–78; S. P. Cerasano, 'The Master of the Bears in art and enterprise', *Medieval and Renaissance Drama in England*, vol. 5, 1991, pp195–209.

[2] see page 26, note 3.

[3] R. A. Foakes and R. T. Rickert 1961 (page 16, note 13), Muniment 22, line 7, p307.

[4] S. Blatherwick and A. Gurr 1992 (page 16, note 16), p321, fig.4. It should be noted that in an appendix to this article John Orrell prefers a Globe diameter of 32.77m (100ft); see also Orrell, 'Beyond the Rose: design problems for the Globe reconstruction', *New Issues in the Reconstruction of Shakespeare's Theatre*, Franklin J. Hildy (ed) 1990 (page 10, note 2), pp95–118.

[5] see page 26, note 3.

[6] W. Lambarde, *Perambulations in Kent*, 1596, cited in E. K. Chambers 1923 (page 15 note 1), vol. II, p359; T. Platter, ibid, vol. II, p365; see also A. Gurr, 'The bare island', *Shakespeare Survey* vol. 47, 1994, pp29–43, especially pp40–43.

[7] For the Hope see W. W. Greg 1931 (page 16, note 14), Muniment 49, p20, lines 29–33. What appears to be a stair turret is seen at the north-east angle of the Swan: R. A. Foakes 1985 (page 53, note 5), no. 13, pp 24–25. This would fall within the area which was unexcavated at the Rose. The existence of stair turrets at the Theatre cannot be confirmed by a careful examination of an engraving showing the building of about 1597, see Foakes 1985, pp8–9.

[8] The documentary evidence for external staircase turrets at the Fortune, and the Globe, is ambiguous; 'wth suchelike steares Conveyances & divisions *wthoute* & wthin as are made and Contryved in and to the late erected Plaiehowse ... Called the Globe' (W. W. Greg 1931, Muniment 22 p5, lines 29–31) [my italics]. No stair turret is seen on any of the engravings of the first Globe, cf. Foakes 1985, pp11, 13, 14, 17, 19. A rectangular brickwork structure against an angle of the outer wall of the Globe was uncovered in 1989 and initially interpreted as the stair turret

from the second Globe: A. Gurr, 'A first doorway into the Globe', *Shakespeare Quarterly*, vol. 41, no. 1, Spring 1990, pp97–100, but this identification is now open to reinterpretation; S. Blatherwick, pers comm. On stair turrets and audience entrances see now A. Gurr 1994 (page 64, note 6), pp140–43. Here, however, much of the evidence is questioned, for Gurr does not admit the possibility that stair turrets may have been added to some playhouses after their original construction.

[9] The Red Lion stage was recorded as 12 by 9.14m or 109.68m^2 ('fortye foote by thyrty foot' or 1200sq ft), S. Loengard 1983 (page 15, note 2), p309; that at the Boar's Head was 12.07m by about 7.6m or 91.75m^2 (39ft 7in. by about 25ft or 990sq ft), H. Berry, *The Boar's Head Playhouse*, Associated University Presses, Cranford New Jersey, 1986, p108; the width of the Fortune stage was 13.1m (43ft) wide and in 'breadth to extend to the middle of the yarde', W. W. Greg 1931 (page 16, note 14), Muniment 22, p5, lines 35–37; the interior, the yard, was to be 16.76m (55 ft) square, ibid, lines 17–18, thus suggesting the said breadth of the stage to be about 8.38m (27ft 6in); (therefore 13.1 x 8.38m or 109.78m^2/43 x 27ft 6in. or 1182 sq ft).

[10] John H. Astington, 'The origins of the *Roxana* and *Messalina* illustrations', *Shakespeare Survey*, vol. 43, 1991, pp149–69, who shows that these illustrations were not based on any one particular theatre.

[11] H. Berry 1986 (note 9, above) pp35, 108–9.

[12] C. W. Wallace 1913 (page 15, note 4), pp69–70, 76; H. Berry, 'Aspects of the design and use of the first public playhouse', pp29–45 in H. Berry (ed.) 1979 (page 15, note 4), p32.

[13] For the relevant passages in the Fortune and Hope contracts, see page 53, notes 8 and 9. A poem on the burning of the Globe in 1613, *Execration upon Vulcan* by Ben Jonson, includes the lines:

See the World's ruins! Nothing but the piles
Left, and wit since to cover it with tiles.

(cited in E. K. Chambers 1923 [page 15, note 1], vol. II, p422.) However, whether these piles were literary or factual has not been determined by the Globe excavations, which did not penetrate to a depth where they might have been encountered.

[14] The Globe reference is construed from Platter's visit to 'the strewn roof-house' on the south bank, cited in E. K. Chambers 1923, vol. II, p365. The Fortune contract mentions 'Tyle' over the stage cover and among the general building materials needed (W. W. Greg 1931, Muniment 22, p5, line 44; p6, line 74) but the Hope contract states 'Englishe tyles all the upper Rooffe of the saide Plaie house' (ibid, Muniment 49, p21, lines 60–61).

Playing at the Rose

T HE 1587 AGREEMENT states that the purpose of the building was to host performances of 'any playe or enterlude'[1]. A different play was put on six days a week, with the prohibition on Sunday playing often being broken. In 1599 Thomas Platter recorded that playing commenced at about two o'clock in the afternoon[2], and a poem by John Davies a few years later suggests that the playhouses were open until six in the evening[3]. Nevertheless, probably the performance of a play took less time then than it does today and Paul Hentzner in 1598 said that after the performance of a comedy or tragedy there were a 'variety of dances accompanied by excellent music and the excessive applause of those that are present.'[4]. That music was performed at the Rose seems clear from Henslowe's accounts, which state that in 1598 he lent some money to the Admiral's Men 'to bye a basse viall & other enstrements for the companey', while another loan the following year was for them 'to buy 2 trumpettes'[5].

Actors who visited the site during the excavations were impressed by the simplicity and size of the stage, and remarked on the intimate relationship that must have existed between the players and the audience. This proximity would have ensured that each whisper, nuance and gesture portrayed on the stage was appreciated by the audience. The size of the building and the resonance enhanced by its wooden superstructure would have provided great experience for the actors honing their skills. Despite a growing interest in spectacle, great stress was laid on the audience's power of imagination, much emphasis being on the rich language of the words delivered. Edward Alleyn's stentorian style of delivery would have been powerfully felt in the small Rose[6].

Playwrights usually wrote for companies rather than for specific venues, and different stages could be adapted as necessary. A large body of plays known to have been performed at the Rose survives, and an analysis of staging directions has been discussed by many scholars[7]. However, such material should be used with caution, since the texts as we have them today were almost certainly printed some time after their original performances.

Henslowe's accounts of 1598 list gaudy and expensive costumes and stage properties belonging to the Admiral's Men. These include a cauldron, used in the The Jew of Malta, a cage, used in Tamburlaine, a rock, mossy banks, and a Hell's mouth for Dr Faustus[8]. Nevertheless these may have been minor, easily removable items, as the stage at the Rose would have been too small for elaborate staging devices[9].

The Rose may well have had a gallery or balcony in the first floor of the tiring-house facade, as seen on the drawing of the Swan. Internal stairs would have given access to this. There are numerous directions for action to take place upon and against walls, ramparts and towers, as well as at windows. When Venus was to be let down from the top of the stage in Greene's early Alphonsus of Aragon, she may have been lowered from this point. Apart from this gallery's dramatic use it was perhaps also here that musicians performed the 'enterludes' and the 'musicke' decreed for Dr Faustus.

Behind the stages of both Phases it is probable that there was a curtain, or 'arras' hung across door openings in the tiring-house facade to facilitate entrance on to the stage and behind which scenes would be 'discovered'. Part II of Tamburlaine 'the arras is drawne' and Munday's Downfall of Robert, Earl of Huntingdon of about 1598 include a part 'within the curteines'. References to 'the other door' indicate that there may have been at least two, and the angled scenae frons, in both phases of the Rose, would suggest three. The shape of the stage could therefore accommodate processions and the like 'passing over the stage'[10].

Wickham's arguments that trap doors were not required by plays performed at the Rose would seem to be supported by the restricted height below the Rose stage[11]. Directions from The Silver Age by Thomas Heywood suggest that characters such as devils would be able to emerge directly into the yard from under the stage through the supporting timber[12]. Part of the yard itself, just in front of the stage, may also have been used for some of the dramatic action[13]. There can be no proof for this from the excavations, but there was certainly no indication that any part of the yard was separately enclosed.

Once permanent pillars had been inserted for the new roof, they could also have been utilised as posts or trees, despite being close to the stage front. It is almost certainly one of these that was addressed by a character in Henry Porter's Two Angry Women of

Abingdon of about 1598: 'A plague on this poast, I would the carpenter had bin hangd that set it up for me' as he stumbled about in the dark field of the story.

Various directions refer to objects being raised and lowered from the new roof, such as an empty throne in Marlowe's *Dr Faustus*, or a sword in Lodge's and Greene's *A Looking Glass for London*, of 1592. In June 1595 Henslowe further paid seven pounds and two shillings (£7.10) for 'carpenters work & mackinge the throne in the hevenes'[14]. Perhaps this meant that with greater difficulty, even people could also be lowered, as in Heywood's *The Silver Age* where 'Jupiter discends in a cloude', or Haughton's *Englishmen for my Money* of 1598, where someone is lowered in a basket. However, when Absalom was to be raised by the hair in the 1602 performance of Peele's *David and Bathsheba*, Henslowe had to pay for 'poleyes & worckmanship'[15].

Notes

1 R. A. Foakes and R. T. Rickert 1961 (page 16, note 13), Muniment 16, line 43, pp305–6.

2 Cited in E. K. Chambers 1923 (page 15, note 1), vol. II, p365.

3 'He goes to the Gyls, where he doth eate till one,
Then sees a Play til sixe, and sups at seaven,'

From *In Fuscum*, epigram no. 39, cited in A. Gurr 1992 (page 15, note 1), p7.

4 Cited in J. D. Wilson 1949 (page 16, note 15), p207.

5 R. A. Foakes and R. T. Rickert 1961, f52v, p102; ibid, f67v, p130.

6 On Alleyn's acting style, see A. Gurr, 'Who strutted and bellowed', *Shakespeare Survey*, vol. 16, 1963, pp95–102. A detailed discussion of the stage is to be found in Bowsher (forthcoming, page 27, note 12).

7 On the Rose plays, see Rhodes 1978 (page 15, note 7); S. McMillin, 'Staging at the Rose', chapter 6 in *The Elizabethan Theatre and the Book of Sir Thomas Moore*, Cornell University Press, 1987; A. Gurr 1990 (page 26, note 11).

8 R. A. Foakes and R. T. Rickert 1961, pp316–25; C. C. Rutter 1984 (page 26, note 3), Doc. 65, pp133–7.

9 Suggested in S. McMillin 1987 (note 7, above), p132.

10 See A. Nicoll, 'Passing over the stage', *Shakespeare Survey*, vol. 12, 1959, pp47–55.

11 G. Wickham has twice emphasised this point: 'Notes on the staging of Marlowe's plays', chapter 7 in *Shakespeare's Dramatic Heritage*, Routledge, London, 1969, pp125–6; 'Heavens, machinery, and pillars in the theatre and other early playhouses', pp1–15 in Berry (ed) 1979 (page 15, note 4), p4. However, a trap seems to have been incorporated at the Red Lion of 1576, where 'a certayne space or voyde part of the same stage [was] left unboarded', S. Loengard 1983 (page 15, note 2), p309. It may be noted that a trapdoor is seen on the Messalina frontispiece; John H. Astington, *Shakespeare Survey*, vol. 43, 1991, p154 (page 65, note 10).

12 A. Nicoll 1959 (note 10, above), p51. The identification of this play with the Rose is disputed; see S. McMillin 1987 (note 7, above), p115, note 2.

13 Such a use of the yard has been argued by J. W. Saunders, 'Vaulting the rails', *Shakespeare Survey*, vol. 7, 1954, pp69–81; J. L. Simmons, 'Elizabethan stage practice and Marlowe's *The Jew of Malta*', *Renaissance Drama*, vol. 4, 1972, pp93–104; A. Nicoll 1959 (note 10, above).

14 R. A. Foakes and R. T. Rickert 1961, f2v, p7.

15 ibid, f116v, p217.

Postcript

notes and drawings by C. Walter Hodges

The lost playhouses

THE FAMOUS PUBLIC 'PLAYHOWSSES' of Elizabethan and Jacobean London, the Rose, the Swan, the Globe, the Fortune and others, had a lifetime altogether of nearly seventy years, during which time they fostered the development of one of the most famous periods in the whole history of the theatre. Yet when they had all disappeared, abolished by Parliament during the Civil War, with the last of them being pulled down soon after in 1656, they left behind them little or no record to show what they had actually looked like, and not for more than a hundred years thereafter was anybody very interested to find out. Then, in 1780, Edmund Malone, a scholar seeking to throw light on the (by then) obscure subject of Shakespeare's stagecraft, collected and published some contemporary accounts of the old theatres of the poet's time, together with some speculations of his own about them and how they had worked; and with that began the long search for the true nature of the theatres for which Shakespeare and his fellow dramatists had written their plays.

Pictures of Elizabethan theatres were very few and, such as they were, unsatisfactory, and a history of theatrical presentation apart from the literature of plays did not exist. It was not until 1888 — one hundred years after Malone — that a single drawing, the sketch of the interior of the Swan theatre drawn in 1596 from the on-the-spot 'observations' of a Dutch visitor to London, was found and published. Its uncompromising plainness, so unlike anything expected as a background for Shakespeare, was found rather disappointing, but it helped to start the practice of making conjectural reconstructions of Shakespearean theatres, which has been pursued with scholarship and imagination until the present day. Not since the last of those old theatres was demolished in 1656 had there been sight of any part, neither stick nor stone, of any one of them that could help to confirm any of the conjectures that had been made about them, or even to prove that any of them had ever really existed. Then in February 1989 the actual foundations of the Rose theatre, which Shakespeare himself had known and maybe even worked in, were brought to light on Bankside, on the ground where it once had stood.

Questions of reconstruction

It may be asked whether, after so long, the emergence of this new and remarkable source of evidence upsets or supports the conjectural pictures of Shakespeare's theatre that have been so studiously put together without it. Julian Bowsher, the archaeologist responsible for the find, has already noted in this account a number of differences between what the conjecturing specialists had advised him to look out for, and what in fact he found or did not find on the ground. There were of course many surprises, but nothing to discredit the ideas that have guided the principle of conjecture as a whole. As Julian Bowsher has said, the Rose has emphasised that 'clearly there was no paradigmatic "Shakespearean theatre"', and in this the trend of recent scholarship agrees with him. The playhouses differed from each other with the development of the theatrical profession. The Rose may be taken as an example of this development because it was in itself a theatre in the process of change; one building in two phases of a developing style. Therefore a picture of it must surely be useful for study: or, rather, since one of its surprises has been to find that only five years after it was first put up it was partly taken down to be refashioned and enlarged, it needs not one picture but two.

It must be remembered that the excavation of the Rose is not at present complete. Until the foundations remaining still buried on the eastern side (nearly one-third) are revealed, any reconstructional picture of the whole building must be considered as only provisional. It may be assumed, however, that the rest of the polygonal shape of the foundations will in general complete the pattern shown in the excavation already made (although, even so, those foundations have shown themselves to be not entirely regular, and there may yet be other surprises in store). Nevertheless, I have attempted to show the Rose theatre in both its forms, Phases I and II. These pictures are, of course, a personal interpretation; but to explain my imaginary view in the light of present historical research and of the facts as they have been revealed at the site, I here append some brief notes of my procedure.

Phase I (1587–1592)

FORMATION

In its first phase the theatre was laid out on a plot of ground 28.67m (94ft) square, as a rough polygon having, it seems, fourteen sides. Its timber framing was prefabricated away from the site, and carried in to be erected on foundations which were being prepared for it, section by section. Whether or not the main horizontal timbers were originally supposed to have been cut to standard lengths, it seems in the event they were not, but were subject to variations in the laying of the foundation courses set out for them. It is because of such irregularities as this that the true size and shape of the building cannot be calculated until all its remains are finally brought to light.

ACCESS

In the drawings shown here, the main entrance to the theatre is assumed to have been placed centrally on its south side, leading directly from Maiden Lane, the main east to west highway from Southwark. Between Maiden Lane and the theatre ran an important drainage ditch, which the theatre audiences had to cross by a footbridge. Through the door they entered a yard open to the sky but surrounded by three tiers of roofed galleries. In this first phase of the theatre the yard was raked downwards at a pitch of about seven degrees overall, towards the stage at the far side opposite the entrance. The yard had a surface of mortar. Access from the yard to the galleries seems in other theatres to have been by steps up from the yard (see the Swan theatre), but in Phase I of the Rose

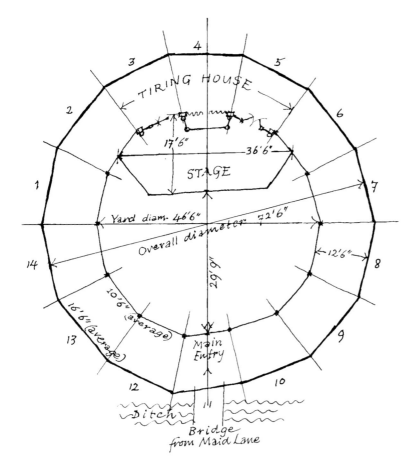

Reconstructed plan of the Rose theatre, Phase I.

there is no indication of this, and the bottom gallery may here have been entered from the main door, with stairs beyond leading to the upper galleries. Exact positions for these stairways cannot yet be determined, but some are indicated here in my drawings, in the oblique corners of the auditorium which we may suppose were least favourable for viewing the stage.

There was a backstage (tiring-house) door for the actors, and it is likely there were others, about which we may guess but have at present no knowledge.

ROOF

There is good evidence that most, if not all, the earlier theatres outside the boundaries of the City were roofed with thatch, and it was so at the Rose. Residues of its thatching were found in the excavation.

GALLERIES

The Rose's proprietor, Philip Henslowe, later built another theatre, the Fortune, in 1600 for which his contract with the builder still exists, giving specifications for the heights of its three galleries. These measurements are sometimes taken as a standard prescription, and so might seem appropriate here. But the Rose theatre was smaller than the Fortune, and the Fortune's gallery heights, if closed around the Rose's narrower circumference, would, I have thought, give an awkwardly steep and cramped view down onto the stage. For this reconstruction therefore, I reduced the gallery heights a little from those of the Fortune, although as always this interpretation may be modified by any subsequent analysis.

The Fortune contract specifies that seating is to be built in its galleries but it is assumed that here at the Rose provision was made for both standing and sitting, giving two or three rows of benches at the front of the galleries, and standing space at the back, which allowed also for a general flow of movement by the audience around the theatre. The yard was used only and entirely for a standing audience.

AUDIENCE

It may be estimated that for Phase I of the Rose, with a well-filled house, and allowance of reasonable room for entrances and passages, the galleries all together might hold, seated and standing, about 1100 persons. For the yard, an experiment conducted with actual persons standing closely together in a measured space, has calculated a capacity of just over 500. Broadly, therefore, we may estimate a crowd total of some 1600, having room enough to push around. Densely crowded there might be more. In addition there would have been a small number of distinguished or wealthier patrons occupying the private gentlemens' rooms near the stage.

THE STAGE

The plan and size of the stage has been revealed in the foundations, but its height above the ground has to be estimated from its viewing position among the audience, and its mode of use. For example, in theatres such as the Globe, there are known requirements in its plays for the use of stage trapdoors, which would thus require a certain amount of headroom for movement of people below the stage. The evidence of the plays given at the Rose in Phase I does not itself suggest any need for this; but if it did it would require a stage standing fairly high off the ground. (There is no sign of digging down for headroom, which the muddy nature of the site here suggests might in any case be unsuitable).

At the same time, a stage with a standing audience all round it needs to be high. At the Rose therefore I have supposed a stage height of 1.52m (5ft), which allows for a standing audience all round without their obstructing the view for those seated in the bottom galleries. I have supposed that the stage itself, like all stages of the time of which we have any knowledge, was supported on wooden posts, which would have been set into sleeper beams laid along the foundation walls prepared for them; but because of a need to keep the underneath of the stage reasonably well aired, I have here supposed it was not permanently closed in with boards, but was hung or tied round with coloured cloth or canvas, which could be removed or brailed up as necessary. The floor of the stage itself is shown strewn over with rushes, which was customary.

THE TIRING-HOUSE

The actors' backstage area (tiring-house) and its frontage onto the stage here occupies three bays of the theatre's polygon on all three gallery levels. This area must have been very crowded. As time went on it cannot have provided room enough for its many purposes, such as backstage preparations, management offices, actors' dressing-room spaces, wardrobe hanging and storage, properties large and small, and all the accumulating gear of a rapidly-growing profession. Repertory theatres like the Rose never have enough room for storage. It is very likely that the need to expand here was a major factor in the later decision to enlarge the whole theatre (see Phase II).

The structural features of the tiring-house frontage can only be conjectured from analysing the special requirements of plays presented at the Rose, taken in the context of the known theatrical and spectacular practices of the time. Here I show, at stage level, three openings from backstage, fitted with doors and/or curtains; at the next level a range of window openings (sometimes needed for plays or perhaps by privileged spectators), with an open central space, here built forward a little like a balcony, which was sometimes needed as an 'upper stage'; and above that another opening, high up, where, in some plays gods or divine messengers might appear

THE ROSE THEATRE

*Reconstructed view of the
Rose theatre, Phase I.*

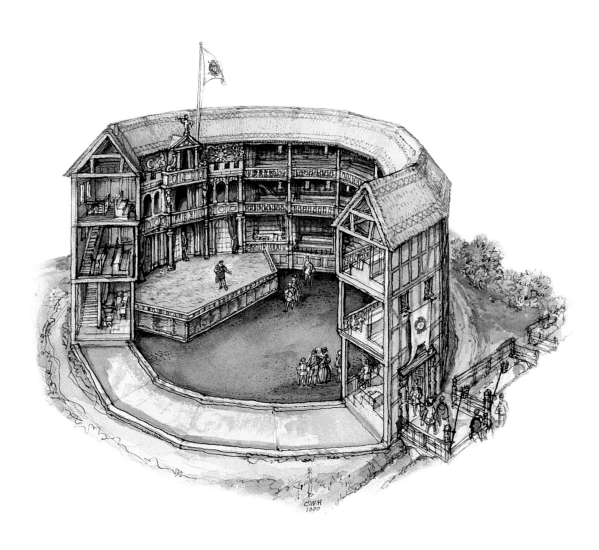

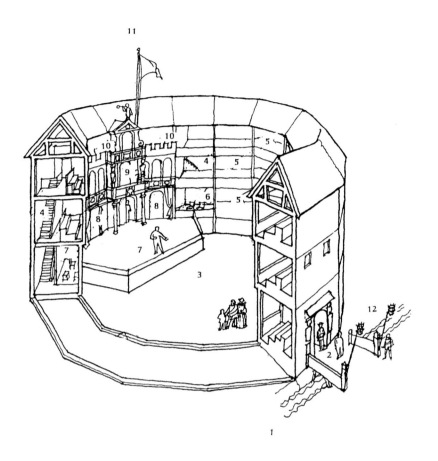

Cutaway showing the features in Phase I

KEY

1 *Ditch along Maiden Lane*
2 *Main door*
3 *Yard for 'groundlings' (standing audience)*
4 *Possible positions for stairs to upper galleries*
5 *Public galleries*
6 *Gentlemen's rooms*
7 *Stage*
8 *Doors onto stage from tiring-house and a third opening with curtains between them, sometimes used for scenes needing prepared furnishings and effects*
9 *Upper stage area with balcony, and window openings at sides*
10 *Heavens area*
11 *Flagstaff, flying flag to announce performance that day*
12 *Cressets*

as if in the heavens.

Also at that same level there is a row of simulated battlements, to give the effect of a castle, since at the time it was popular in plays to present battle scenes, with sieges and assaults upon defended cities. Behind these painted battlements I have supposed there might have been a gutter. Normally with a thatched roof gutters are not used, and here round about the gallery eaves none are shown. Over the stage, with all its painted decoration, it would have been wise to protect the painting against rainwater shedding from the roof. In the excavations below the tiring-house frontage a large wooden drain was found, just where it might have been fed by a down-pipe from such a gutter behind the 'battlements'. During this first phase of the building there appears to have been no roof or other superstructure over the stage, such as was added in Phase II.

Phase II (1592–1603)

ENLARGEMENT

At some time towards the end of 1591 the Rose theatre closed its doors, and the building was given over to a large-scale alteration that may have taken some time to complete. The entire northern half of it seems to have been dismantled, roof, galleries and all, down to the ground, and rebuilt, it seems, on a new foundation line in a new, expanded form.

According to the capacity experiment the enlargement gave space for an additional 150 spectators in the yard, with proportionate increases in the galleries, though this cannot be properly computed until after the full excavation of the eastern side. The enlargement would have given better, that is wider and less cramped, sightlines all round, and certainly must have provided additional working and storage space backstage. Henslowe records at this time a payment for 'making a penthouse shed at the tiring-house door', but this was likely to have been a weather-roof or lobby, rather than for accommodation.

The stage itself was made rather wider and moved back to a new line 1.98m (6ft 6in.) farther north. The more spacious yard now lost its slight rake and its mortared surface – both of which had evidently been unsatisfactory – and was levelled up and resurfaced with an aggregate of cinders and nutshells.

RE-ALIGNMENT

A change of alignment in the northern half of the excavated foundations shows how the original polygon had been opened out. There is now little trace in the ground to show what was done in the northern half, although there are certain significant indications, and also a reasonable deduction to be made from considering the question of what happened to the dismantled framework of the original building. This amounted to a great quantity of valuable oak timbers, ready cut and joined for the outer wall-frames, the gallery frontages and the trusses, rafters and other timbers of the roof. All these frames if carefully taken down would be suitable for re-use, as would most of the floorboards and other fittings. It is unlikely that so much costly material would have been cast aside to make way for the purchase of new.

For the Rose, with some possible refashioning of certain joints

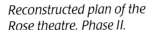

*Reconstructed plan of the
Rose theatre, Phase II.*

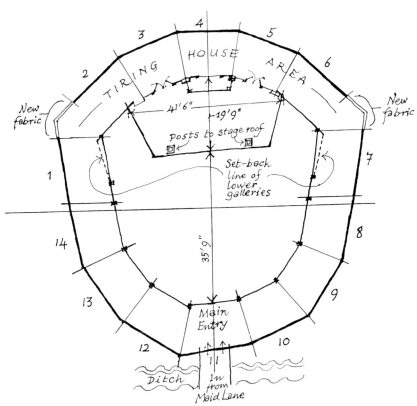

and perhaps new posts in some places, but with not much additional work otherwise, the existing frames from the first phase of the building could have been moved out and re-erected farther back. At the end corners of the tiring-house north wall the limits of the new alignment are clearly defined by a change of angle in the foundations. The additional material needed to make up the entire length of the enlarged building was a very small proportion of the whole, about 3.05m (10ft) on each side.

There is a curious irregularity in the Phase II foundation line of the inner wall frontage of the galleries, in the bays I have numbered 1 and 7. Here the foundation lines narrow slightly towards their northern end, so that the inner and outer walls of the bay are not parallel. Whatever the reason for it may have been, this narrowing is unlikely to have occurred at the roof level. It would have been necessary in re-using the roof trusses to keep the span of the gallery roofing constant and parallel throughout. Therefore at some stage the irregularity made at the foundation line must have corrected itself. In the reconstruction drawing I have shown this correction

THE ROSE THEATRE

*Reconstructed view of the
Rose theatre, Phase II.*

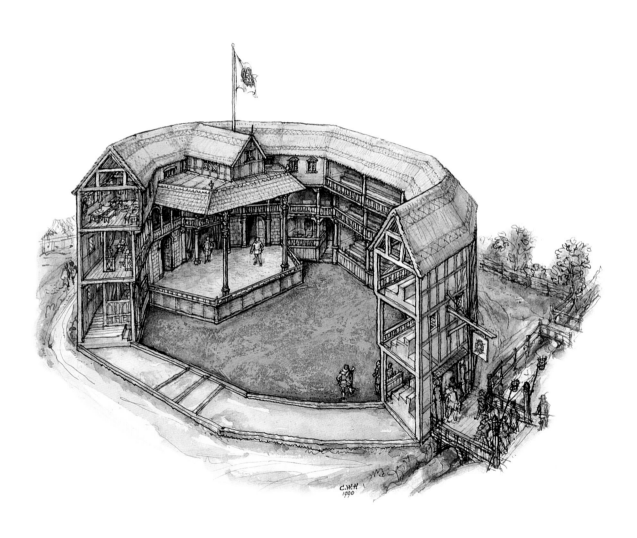

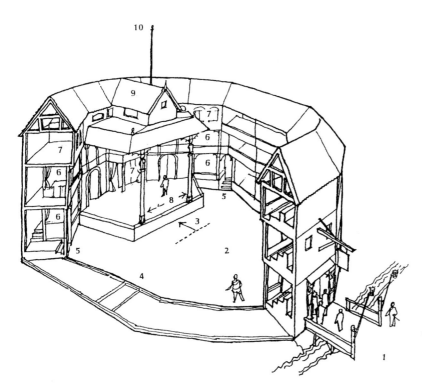

Cutaway showing the features in Phase II

KEY

1 *Entrance from Maiden Lane*
2 *Yard levelled up and newly surfaced*
3 *Stage*
4 *Position of access from yard (on each side) to galleries and stairways*
5 *Possible position of another doorway from yard to tiring-house, boxes and galleries*
6 *Gentlemen's rooms*
7 *Enlarged tiring-house*
8 *Posts to support the heavens*
9 *House for hoisting machine*
10 *Flagstaff; no flag flying signifies no performance for that day*

happening under the top gallery, where from the narrowed formation below it is brought out and supported on corbells.

STAGE AND STAGE COVER

The stage for the newly-enlarged building was itself made slightly larger, but I have supposed it was kept at its original 1.52m (5ft) height, and closed round with removable canvas or hangings, as before. In the excavated foundations of this new stage were discovered the footings for two large posts or pillars set in line just behind the front of the stage. The visual character of these posts deserves brief discussion. Their purpose was to support the front of a roof and another piece of superstructure over the stage. These were now installed to serve the growing elaboration and mechanical technique of these early public theatres. The roof itself may be presumed to have followed the shape of the stage beneath it, as I have shown; but it has to be considered that a more rectangular shape, not so nicely matching the shape below, might have been simpler to construct.

In any case the formation of the roof and its attachment to the upper storey of the tiring-house at the back, would make it unsuitable for the thatching used on roofs everywhere else in the building. Therefore in my drawing it is shown covered on its forward slopes with wooden shingles, some of which were found in the demolition debris in front of the stage. Together with the stage roof there stood a small hut-like structure built against the main roof of the tiring-house, as is clearly shown in Norden's depiction of the Rose in his panorama of 1600.

This little structure presumably contained the hoisting machinery for 'the throne in the heavens' which Henslowe installed in 1595. Seated on this throne an actor dressed as a divine personage could be lowered to the stage through an opening in the stage ceiling. This ceiling in the theatrical language of the time was called 'the heavens', and was thought to have been of boards painted blue and decorated with clouds, stars, figures of the zodiac, etc. At the Rose excavation a great deal of fallen plaster was found in this area, which may have come from the stage ceiling; but it was all entirely without colour and it would seem that the Rose heavens was of unpainted plaster.

STAGE POSTS

The discovery that the two heavens-supporting posts, which must have been substantial, were placed at front of the stage, between the audience and the actors, is more than a little disturbing to modern notions of good visibility in the design of stages. Such posts there certainly were on the Elizabethan stages, but if the Swan theatre drawing is to be believed — in spite of its eccentricities of perspective — these were sometimes if not generally placed well back from the front. The Rose discovery, however, suggests that this belief may now need to be reconsidered. To make my own reconciliation with new facts, therefore, I am suggesting the following design for the Rose. Because posts in the classical style as at the Swan (bases, capitals, painted marbling, etc) would certainly have been over-dominating here, I suggest instead that their style should be of plain timber in keeping with the general nature of the rest of the building, and of a darkish colour. (Pale colours in this position would be reflective, and bedazzle a view of the stage.)

At the same time I think the two posts, being unavoidable presences on the scene — personalities as it were in their own right — would have characteristics suitable to the style and atmosphere of a theatre of that time. I have therefore imagined them as being posts of dark oak, 0.25m (10in.) square, chamfered, and carved at the top with heroic half-figures in the Late Elizabethan style – say, of some legendary king and queen, or of London's tutelary giants Gog and Magog. (Henslowe at his Fortune theatre had 'carved proportions called Satyrs ... set on the top' of all 'the principal and main posts of the ... frame and stage forward'). Perhaps at the Rose the 'carved proportions' of legendary figures which I have imagined on the tops of the two stage posts might have been picked out here and there with colour, perhaps even with some gilding. I ought to stress, however, that this and other such details of ornamentation which I have described or shown in my pictures are what may be called 'educated guesswork' of my own; though I think it would be wrong in itself not to try to provide such guesses about the characteristic appearance of this theatre as a whole.

The passage quoted above from the Fortune contract about 'the principal posts of the frame and stage forward' has been familiar to scholars for two hundred years, but I think never in all that time has any reconstruction of the Fortune attempted to show that theatre with posts standing at the forward edge of the stage. 'Stage forward' has always been conveniently assumed to imply the position shown in the Swan drawing: on the stage, but forward of the tiring-house frontage. Now, however, be it welcome or unwelcome, we are obliged to consider whether or not 'stage forward' in Henslowe's Fortune contract may have meant the same forward arrangement of the posts as we now find at his previous theatre, the Rose. The excavation of the Rose is proving to be a mine of new evidences far beyond anything expected.

EXIT

Outside the theatre, at the Maiden Lane footbridge end, I have shown two iron 'cressets' on poles. These are fire-baskets, which, being packed with flammable material, were lighted to show the roadway on dark evenings. Henslowe's accounts show that plays were being performed at the Rose all through the winter, and I have supposed that for audiences leaving the play at the end of the afternoon's performance – all public theatre performances had to be given by daylight and finished as the evening closed in – it would be necessary to light the way for them at least as far as the other side of the bridge.

Selective Glossary

Archaeological, architectural and theatrical terms

beam slot: a narrow trench dug to receive foundation beams; archaeologically, usually indicates that the beams have disappeared.

beneficial deposit: in many societies, an animal or body part has been buried in the foundations of a building as a good-luck charm; note 7 on page 57 suggests further reading.

butted up: a later addition to a structure, lying next to the original and in contact with it, but not integrated with its construction.

construction cut: an area dug into the ground to receive specific elements of structural foundations.

cover: the roof, including but not limited to, the **heavens**.

destruction deposits or **destruction layers:** archaeological remains, indicative of destruction.

demolition debris: *see above,* **destruction deposits/layers**.

dump: used here to indicate an archaeological layer.

fill: used here to indicate an archaeological layer.

gentlemen's rooms: used by some scholars who distinguish them from **lords' rooms**, but here used interchangeably to denote areas similar to boxes in modern theatres, which were probably more expensive than standing room in the open yard.

heavens: the roof over the stage, more specifically its underside, and perhaps painted to represent the 'heavens', from which gods or other characters in the plays were seen to descend by means of stage machinery in the later Tudor and Stuart theatres.

hut: a small structure over the roof of the theatre, possibly to house stage machinery; *see* **heavens**. Such a structure is shown in Norden's panorama of 1600.

ingressus: an internal entrance way within a building.

jetty: the projection of an upper storey beyond a lower one, formed by the timber beams and joists which support it.

levelling course: a build-up of layers in order to establish a new level height for a new activity, usually of a constructional nature.

lords' rooms: *see above,* **gentlemen's rooms**.

medieval period: the period spanning approximately 700–1485.

pargetted: decorative plaster work on timber, common on buildings in the time of the Rose.

piles: upright posts, driven vertically into the ground in order to provide strength and security to a building's foundations.

post holes: an archaeological term for a void in the ground, originally dug to accommodate an upright timber post or stake from which this timber has usually vanished; it is identified by having a different fill from the surrounding layer of earth.

rescue excavation: archaeological excavation before building work which might otherwise destroy buried remains.

revetted: having a retaining wall or fence.

robbed: *see below,* **robber trench**.

robber trench: archaeologists can identify where building materials or walls have been removed for re-use elsewhere from negative traces which remain, just as they can with **post holes**.

Roman period: the Romans occupied Britain from AD 43–410.

scenae frons: used by Vitruvius to describe the building behind the stage of a theatre; at the Rose, this incorporated the tiring-house.

section: a vertical exposure of archaeological deposits or layers; *also,* a drawing to illustrate this.

sealed: an archaeological layer or feature which has been completely covered by another layer above it, so that it is not mixed with other layers and its integrity is preserved.

sellynge: interpreted here as plastering, for example of a wall surface; see note 26, page 54.

slot: archaeologically, a small exploratory trench.

stratigraphy: borrowed from geologists by archaeologists, to describe the layering of deposits and the time sequence of their deposition; basically the uppermost layers must be later in time than those below, although there may be intrusive elements such as pits which were dug through a number of earlier layers.

superstructure: that part of a building above the foundations (*or, archaically,* its substructure); generally, the part above ground level is usually the greater part of the building, and it is precisely this part which is unlikely to have survived archaeologically.

thrust: (*of walls*) their tension or stress in an engineering sense; *also used* of the projection of the stage beyond the ***scenae frons*** into the yard which accommodated the majority of the audience.

tiring-house: the backstage area, enclosed as a room or series of rooms, where the actors could change their costumes (attire themselves); the equivalent of the green room today.

Index

Picture credits